~~Falling~~ *Failing* in love

How failed relationships can lead to love at its finest

Juliette Sweeney

To my husband, Liam, for cheering me on from day one and showing me such love that has created the foundation for this book. For my baby girl, Inaya, who was all the motivation I needed to finally finish writing this book.

Introduction

At the time of writing this, I am a 27-year-old who has been married for two and a half years, with a beautiful (nearly) seven-month old baby girl that I'm blessed to be able to call mine.

Since my childhood, I've had an interest in understanding love and relationships. While we were dating, myself and my husband would lead presentations and workshops on this topic. Our aim was to provide a platform for discussion and personal growth.

With plenty of experience writing professionally, words have always come naturally to me. I wanted to be able to use this skill to reach people and encourage them in some way.

From blogging to journaling, writing a book on love and relationships has been an (overdue) long-term goal of mine that I am proud to finally be able to put in the hands of readers like you.

I hope that you are inspired by the following pages, and that you'll also recognise your strength in love despite failure.

Contents

1 · Puzzle Pieces

Him: *"I love you, you know that right?"*

The power that those three little words can have on you is incredible! My frustration eased and I began to reflect. To think that frustration towards my boyfriend could bring out an expression of love was… strange.

I remembered hearing those same three words from an ex-boyfriend, only I didn't feel the same way when he said it. Nope - nothing apart from confusion. I awkwardly responded with, "I appreciate you letting me know", to which he took offence and asked me why I didn't say it back. I asked myself that same question, but I had no answer.

Looking back, I now know that wasn't real love. It sure felt like something similar at the time after I pushed myself into giving the relationship a go, but I've learned since then that love can't be forced. When you're surrounded by so many shallow examples of love, it's no wonder that our understanding of true love can turn out to be the furthest from the truth! Even in the right context, the smallest expressions of raw love are so often taken for granted. Take away the fluff of fancy gifts (as meaningful as they may be), and you'll often find a surprising amount of value in what's left behind.

Have you ever completed a puzzle? There's a sense of satisfaction when you see the picture start to take shape, as you patiently and carefully match the pieces together. Designed to suit various levels of ability, you can choose from easier jumbo-sized puzzles to the complex 500+ piece puzzles. If we're honest, many of us wouldn't have the patience to sit and complete a complex 500+ piece puzzle. Rather than being spurred on by a sense of achievement from seeing the picture slowly take shape, our patience would probably run out very quickly.

Love is a lot like those complex puzzles, and funnily enough most of us react to it in the same way! We want the "jumbo-sized" version of love that looks easy and predictable to us, but once we realise that we've instead stepped into a complex reality that requires more patience than we care to provide, we get frustrated and give up. On the other side of the frustration, you can often nurture the love that you desire by challenging yourself to remain consistent and patient.

As the picture starts to take shape and you understand what love is, your entire perception will change. A healthy relationship will shape both people involved for the better, and slowly yet steadily, you'll create a foundation that can survive the many tests that come with time.

The concept of love and its seemingly endless puzzle pieces have been analysed over the years from every angle possible, but there is still so much to learn. Counsellors still offer advice to couples struggling in their marriages, people who have been hurt are still sceptical of love, and many children are still growing up exposed to a negative example of love at home.

As a little girl, I had so many questions. There was a phase where I was fascinated with the idea of kissing. I would try to draw pictures of people kissing (the key word being "try"). The lips would always end up looking oversized on little faces, with sausage fingers outstretched in delight. I would also play out scenarios with my soft toys, pairing them up and sealing their union with a clumsy kiss. Somehow, a dinosaur and a shark made sense in my mind.

I remember playing with my Barbie dolls too, including the male versions of the dolls; Ken and Steven. It was far easier to act out a relationship with these little plastic people. With their trim figures, stylish clothes and permanently happy expressions, love seemed to happen naturally for my dolls. I mean come on, who would say no to "perfect" proportions and a plastered smile? It all went downhill when I decided to give one of the dolls a haircut with the belief that her long hair would eventually grow back. Even with her hair looking a hot mess after I hacked away at it, my Barbie kept smiling. Unlike Angelica's Cynthia doll from "The Rugrats", I decided my Barbie was no longer attractive with her prickly haircut, so she was sadly out of the running for love. She was still smiling though.

Then along came my Baby Annabelle doll, requiring far more time and attention. She would cry if she was hungry, to which I would feed her with a plastic bottle of milk-less milk, and she would let out a soft burp when she was full. If I made too much noise while she was sleeping, she would start crying again! My younger brother quickly caught on to this, and thought it would be fun to wake her up whenever she was sleeping. Of course I was not impressed, and her consistent cries of upset caused me to do the unthinkable... Yes, I confess! I turned her off. As soon as I discovered the switch beneath the velcro flap attached to her plump body, things became a whole lot more convenient.

Sadly, this convenience didn't play out quite the same way in reality as it did with my demanding baby doll. There was no switch to stop my parents arguing. No amount of milk-less milk could ease the feelings of hurt that were evident within our home. I couldn't do anything but watch and listen, and in my immature mind the sadness just didn't make sense. Surely if mummy and daddy just kissed. Surely if they just had a good night's sleep...

How do you make everything better when you are too young to understand the problems that need solving?

I used to love reading "The Story of Tracy Beaker" by Jacqueline Wilson; a story about the experiences of a girl growing up in a foster home, otherwise known as the "Dumping Ground". I used to imagine myself in a similar situation - escaping my home and making a new life for myself. The stories would allow my imagination to escape, but never once was I brave enough to actually try and run away. I remember imagining it all, but common sense told me that it was far more dangerous to be lost and alone, than to stay where I was.

You may also relate to the challenges of growing up in a divided home. I say divided rather than the typical word, 'broken', as the division was evident between my parents in their marriage, long before they chose to divorce one another. The idea of being 'broken' suggests that there is an opportunity for repair, and as much as I believe that no one is beyond help, not everyone is willing to accept help in the first place. A willingness to change can't be forced, and this is where division takes place.

As an adult with a family of my own, I can look back with a mature perspective on my childhood with empathy for what my parents experienced, but that doesn't mean that my own experience no longer affects me. I try to use my childhood as a springboard to learn from and to hopefully encourage others who have or are experiencing the same, but I'm still learning and encouraging myself in the process. I once heard of the home environment being called a 'greenhouse', and the metaphor stuck with me. I read how from roughly 0-6 years of age, you are taking in everything around you and soaking it straight in without any filter. Beyond this age, the frontal cortex of the brain then becomes that filter. This has a huge impact on your brain and shapes the way you develop relationships both with others and with yourself, as a child and as an adult.

It's unrealistic to expect your past to just go away and no longer have any impact on your future. The key is to be able to accept where you've come from, but recognise that you have the ability to shape your future and choose not *if* your past affects you, but instead to choose *how* it affects you. When something is a trigger to a difficult childhood experience (sometimes without you even realising), it can be the ideal opportunity to learn in that moment and question why you reacted in the way you did, or why those feelings surfaced. The more you can learn and understand yourself, the better you can handle those triggers, to the extent where they strengthen your ability to offer yourself the level of self-care you deserve.

Remember that who you are, past and present, is who someone else will potentially be joining themselves with for life. The better you understand you, the better you can help your partner to do the same. This gives them the ability to offer a welcome source of strength and encouragement when you are feeling vulnerable because they actually *know* you for better or for worse.

The experiences from my childhood are memorable, mainly because they began to shape my perception of love. My immature understanding meant that I was trying to piece together a puzzle with no idea of what the picture was actually supposed to look like. This didn't stop me from trying though. I was determined to understand what was happening, and why it was happening to me in particular.

Thanks to the fact that my mum was always very open and honest with me, combined with a growing relationship with God and the opportunity to experience the world outside of my home, slowly but surely I finally began to understand what the picture *should* look like.

Your thoughts

Take a moment to consider your own childhood experiences, and how they may have shaped your perception of love - good or bad. So much of why we are the way we are can be traced back to our childhood, and I've personally found and continue to find it really helpful to explore how I feel about my past.

Note down any particular experiences that you can think of, and ask yourself the following questions:

1. How did that experience make me feel?
2. Is it still something that is affecting me today, and if so how?
3. If negative, how can I make sure that experience no longer holds me back?
4. If positive, what can I do to use that experience to my advantage?

I wasn't always comfortable addressing my feelings, especially those that related to sad and painful memories, but I know it was and still is exactly what I need to do to live my best quality of life.

2 · Boy Creatures

It was the morning of another day at my primary school, and I was looking forward to it for one reason in particular. It was a special day - a day when love is celebrated! A day where I would hopefully get to experience some of that love for myself...

A couple of days before in class, our teacher had given us the opportunity to make a Valentine's Day card for someone special. It could be for a family member, a special friend, or maybe even someone else in the room! I remember feeling an awkward sense of excitement as I set about making my card. Our teacher had reminded us that it was meant to be a surprise, so we were asked to keep it once completed and give it to the person on the day.

As I cut out heart shapes from the coloured paper and glued them carefully in place, my mind was occupied with the possibility of receiving a card from a certain boy in my class (looking back, I can't even remember who I was making my own card for!) There was no way I was actually going to *tell him* how I felt, as I seemed to lose the ability to speak whenever he spoke to me. There was just something about the way he would smile and lean back on his chair, and the way he would offer me a chewed pen if mine ran out of ink.

My heart skipped into the classroom on this day of love, and I remember people excitedly holding cards that had been placed in their name-trays from not-so-secret admirers. I rushed over to mine and pulled out the tray, eager to get my hands on my very own card, only to find scraps of coloured paper looking back at me. My heart sunk, and I sat back in my seat with a glum sense of disappointment. To make matters worse, *someone else* had received a card from him.

That day I decided that I didn't really like the idea of love after all. Not if it made me feel like that!

One of my earliest memories of "love" happened in nursery when one of the boys ran up to me, grabbed my head and kissed me on the lips. I ran crying to my teacher, completely horrified at such a move from a boy creature! Funny how I went from feelings of such utter disgust at the act of kissing, to complete fascination.

Do you remember the moment when you started feeling attracted to others around you? Maybe it was that boy in your class who you used to find so annoying, or maybe that girl who you always thought of as "one of the lads". Whatever your experience, that moment of realisation not only impacts the way that you treat that person, but it can also influence the way you see yourself. For example, say he or she doesn't seem to feel the same way in return, then you may begin to question if you are "enough" and if you need to change to gain their interest.

This can spill over into adulthood with harmful results, which is why it is so crucial to develop a healthy level of self-esteem as a child. You will then find it easier to filter any negative experiences as constructive lessons learned, even though difficult, without them defining your worth as a person.

As a new parent of a little girl (at the time of writing this), it makes me reflect on the experiences I had navigating boy-land - only now I consider how my mum felt seeing me learning and failing. She may not have been aware of every little detail, but as my mum she had a way of sharing her concerns that always got me thinking. My mum taught me how to think, not what to think, and I've always admired that. Having such a foundation made all the difference to my experience with guys, and it helped me to learn valuable lessons rather than allowing anyone else to limit my belief in my worth.

Of course there were challenging times… It wasn't until my time at university that I got into my first serious relationship. By that time, I won't lie, I wanted a boyfriend! In the past I had spoken to guys with intention, but for one reason or another we hadn't taken the next step. I had always been particular about what I was looking for, and compatibility trumped physical appearance every time. That didn't mean that physical attraction wasn't important to me, but there needed to be something more to that person's character that would boost their physical appeal.

It wasn't until university that I began questioning whether I was being too picky. This uncertainty and desire to be in a relationship led me to meet a great guy during my time there. Unfortunately we weren't compatible in the areas that mattered to me most, which led to our eventual split. Looking back, I know I shouldn't have settled for the sake of my insecurities in finding someone, as I believe we would have made good friends without the drama of being romantically involved. I am thankful for the experience though and I don't regret the relationship, as it taught me so much and encouraged me not to compromise on what I truly wanted in a future spouse.

We ended our relationship graciously, and I'll never forget when he told me "I know you'll find what you're looking for". Thankfully I did, and my husband is proof that there are good men who will exceed your expectations if you refuse to compromise on your values in love.

Love in itself is a fascinating idea. Two people meet despite growing up in different homes with perspectives that are unique to their own families, complete with personal attitudes that have been shaped by unlimited influences, and *still* expect to experience something between them as deep as love. Honestly? It sounds ridiculous!

Just like those arcade machines flaunting expensive prizes, just waiting for you to simply pop in your pound coin and win the game, we all know that in reality the concept is far from simple. How often do people actually win those games? The amount of pound coins that are emptied from the machine each day should tell you something.

How often do people "win" in love? Many end up in the destructive cycle of spending their mental, spiritual and physical wellbeing on the other person, with nothing to show in return. Nobody likes to consider themselves a loser, but the truth is that most of us have lost and still seem to keep losing in love. We've given so much that we feel as though there isn't much left to give.

Is it any surprise that we get tired of hearing about the topic of relationships?

What if there was a guaranteed method that meant that you could finally win in love? *You put in a pound, win the game and the love of your life is yours to claim!* Okay it may not be that easy, but rather than looking at love as a lucky dip, understand that love requires a willingness to learn.

If you had no idea how to drive a car, would you still offer to give someone a lift regardless? I mean, how hard could it be right? What about if the roles were reversed (see what I did there) and someone who had never touched a steering wheel in their life offered you a lift? As mad as it sounds, we do this to each other all the time when we get into relationships and just *feel* our way along, hoping for the best.

When we begin to develop a desire to experience love, we rarely consider actually *learning* what it means to love first. The only prerequisite seems to be that we want to experience love, and off we go! Too many of us learn as we go and define success by the way we feel, but not everything that feels good is good for you…

Your thoughts

What are some questions that you have about love and relationships? Finding the answers will only add to your growth.

Here are a few questions based on your relationship status to get you started, but feel free to be as creative as you want with your own list:

Single

1. What can I do to avoid the wrong relationships?
2. How can I get past being hurt in my previous relationship? *find someone who wants me.*
3. Where should I start if I've never been in a relationship?

Dating

1. How can I build trust with my partner?
2. What are the best ways to be clear on our expectations for this relationship?
3. How do I know if the person I am with is the person I should spend my life with?

Married

1. How should we manage our finances?
2. What should we do to resolve conflict?
3. How do you find a good balance between family, work and leisure?

3 · 100 Questions

Is he/she interested, or do they just see me as a friend?

He/she likes me as more than a friend, but do I feel the same?

Should I ask him/her about making things official between us?

He/she has liked me for a long time, so it's only fair for me to give them a chance, right?

I'm sure you can relate to at least one of these questions. Trying to figure out the other person's next move can cause just as much headache as trying to figure out your own! Those feelings of uncertainty remain, but those questions in your mind need answers…

Sometimes even just the process of working towards a relationship can feel like a minefield, with every step you take throwing up a situation that could make or break your journey with that person. Why can't it be more simple? Why do I feel so confused? Why is love such hard work?!

What some people wouldn't give for a clear route through the confusion, leading to the most incredible relationship that they've been patiently waiting and praying for.

Your relationship shouldn't feel like you are crippled under the weight of endless problems, but no relationship (let alone marriage) is problem-free either. The difference lies in how you deal with any questions or concerns that arise. Healthy communication between you and your partner should create a space where you can talk openly and honestly about anything that is on your mind. If the person who is supposed to know you best can't even be straight with you, or if you feel as though you are carrying around this uncertainty without telling him/her how you really feel, then the very union that is meant to enhance your quality of life will suffocate it instead.

There are some couples who consider the fact that they've never had an argument as a personal achievement. Each couple is entitled to create their own dynamic, but I believe that addressing your differences as a couple is an essential part of any relationship - the key being positive progress. Arguments or disputes shouldn't be filled with aggression, but the frustration voiced should lead to constructive change.

The ability to compromise is a necessity for your relationship, as there will be things that you won't agree on - fact. The sooner you accept this, the sooner you will learn to be patient when faced with opinions that don't reflect your own, rather than being determined to make him/her see things your way. Have you ever considered the thought that you may be wrong? Pete never has!

There is a principle from the book "Love & Respect" by Dr Emerson Eggerichs that says:

"You can be right but wrong at the top of your voice."

When I initially read this, I had to pause and let it sink in. The more I thought about it, the more I began to recognise how significant this idea actually is. No matter how valid the point you are making may be, the *way* that you say it can completely counteract *what* you are saying.

If someone feels attacked by your words, the natural response is to defend themselves. This could either be through attacking you in response, staying silent, or removing themselves from the situation. Whatever the outcome, it's profound to think that all of this can be avoided if you just change your approach.

I grew up seeing a lot of conflict around me. My experience has taught me that shouting at another person does way more harm than good. As a child I would internalise any feelings of hurt or upset, and I often found it difficult to control my emotions in situations of conflict as a result. Although I have learned much since then, I am still learning and I understand the importance of being able to talk about my feelings. As hard as this may be at times, and as much as my emotions may try to take control, I just keep reminding myself how important it is to talk. Not to shout or insult the person in the process, but just to talk...

It sounds so simple, but believe me it's a process, and this is an attitude that many of us fail to practice. Even if you need to take some time to calm down before you talk, it's better to be in the right frame of mind than for your reaction to be based on a surge of emotions.

Within my relationship, I have seen the incredible value in being free to address potential issues without the fear of being attacked. I thank God that we recognise the importance of being completely transparent with one another when it comes to the way we feel, because I have experienced the damage you can do to your relationship by avoiding such issues.

As women, we're more likely to act impulsively based on our emotions. Despite this, it's important to remember that men have emotions and feelings too. They may share them differently, but it saddens me when I see men who are treated like punching bags - as though they can take whatever you throw at them without it affecting them, simply because they are men. The stereotype of a man can be detrimental to their mental health. Men can be just as sensitive, if not more so, than women. The sooner we recognise this truth, the more balanced our approach will be when addressing any problems.

Think about the fact that your closest relationships start off with your parents and siblings. Even when you declared a full blown war against a sibling, with time and maturity it would usually lead to an understanding of how to improve the relationship. You would then know not just what makes them happy, but also what frustrates them or makes them sad.

There are times when it may take may a little while to open up to my partner, but it's encouraging to know that any issues within my marriage can be dealt with constructively. One of us will always do something after that reminds the other of the love we share, as it can be easy to start losing sight of that when you're annoyed!

It's also helpful to note that it takes the willingness of both people to create healthy changes in a relationship. When one person is willing but the other person has no intention of changing, it's almost like trying to row a bout with one oar - you end up going in circles. If you feel as though no matter how hard you are trying nothing is changing, then maybe it's time to check whether he/she is actually rowing along with you. If they were you would be making progress, rather than ending up back where you started…

Some situations will challenge you more than others and the temptation to snap at your partner will always be there, but recognising that there is a better response will help you to develop a more positive, fulfilling relationship.

I remember reading somewhere that you should always remember that you and your partner are on the same team. That has always stayed with me, as when you have your differences you can be swayed into reacting without love, believing that your partner no longer has your best interests in mind. If it's evident that they don't, then you need to take steps to understand why and look at whether you can improve on what you have together. The last thing you should do is consider making a lifelong commitment to someone who has a toxic impact on your quality of life.

With improvement in mind, asking the right questions can lead to a stronger union in your relationship. I think the best inspiration for this comes from our favourite little people! Children aren't afraid to ask questions, and it can be so refreshing to hear how they express themselves.

Even though patience may be required when your entire conversation with a child consists of questions, they have a way of studying the world around them as they really want to learn and understand everything that they experience.

When we get older, we take that ability to be inquisitive for granted. As a child I was constantly told, "If you don't ask, you don't get", and this truth plays out in life in a multitude of ways. When applied to a relationship, the more your attraction grows for your partner, the stronger the desire should be for you to want to learn more about them.

You may be slow to share more of who you are, or you may even be uncomfortable with the idea of letting someone in after previously being hurt, but quality relationships are built on the ability to know and understand your partner better than anyone else. This could take years, and even then something might happen that you think is out of character, but you need to remember that you're both growing together in your relationship and that includes a change in character (hopefully for the better in the long run!) No one is exactly the same person they were 10 years ago, so it's unfair not to leave room to work through tests that will encourage growth with your significant other.

I remember a difficult conversation that I had with my husband not long after we first met, and I say difficult because it made him vulnerable because of how honest he was choosing to be with me. The questions were uncomfortable, but after the conversation it hit me that I was now responsible for his heart. The way that I chose to react had the capacity to either encourage him to open up again in future, or it would be a reason for him to avoid sharing anything else. This was not something to be taken lightly.

From the day I met my husband, I made him my focus of study. Initial intrigue developed into appreciation, which grew into the love that formed our marriage. If I'm honest, it's very easy to lose sight of that strong desire to learn about your partner when you've been with them for a number of years, and feel as though you know enough! It's important to remind yourself (and I'm telling myself too) that there is always more to learn as you face life together. As I mentioned before, no one is the same person throughout their entire life. Showing a continual interest in the person you've chosen to spend your life with will help to keep your love evident across the decades.

In my marriage, we try and keep our relationship with God as the foundation. In the same way that God lovingly wants me to continually learn about who He is, so that I can have a deeper understanding and a more personal relationship with Him, I also recognise the value in continually learning about my husband.

From experience, I strongly believe that it is only through developing a closeness with God that I have been able to understand how to have a healthy relationship. I'm still learning, but this truth has been incredibly significant to my journey in love.

With that understanding, I try to regularly make time for self-reflection. This can include me even questioning *the way* I question myself! It's easy to end up being my own worst enemy by allowing myself to create conclusions without even considering a different perspective.

One of the questions I kept asking myself when I was having issues in a previous relationship was:

"What if you never meet someone else who is willing to commit to you?"

You may relate, as perspectives like this are the very reason why so many of us stay where we are and compromise. It was definitely one of the reasons why I ended up back in the very relationship that I told myself I needed to leave behind, before eventually parting ways for good. Here's a thought… instead of asking, "what if I don't", instead ask, "what if I do!"

Don't allow your questions to create limitations, but explore questions that lead to a fruitful explanation.

Your thoughts

What questions are currently on your mind that seem to be creating a hurdle in your relationship? Take some time to write them down - it can be a great stress-reliever to just get those thoughts out of your head and noted down.

If you have questions for your partner that are especially sensitive, then be aware of how you ask and choose your timing carefully. It may be nice to take a walk with them and share what's on your mind while you have their full attention with minimal distractions.

Try to also take some time for self-reflection, especially if you've never done so before! It can be a truly beneficial experience for your state of mind and overall wellbeing. Here are a few "self" questions to get you started:

1. How do I currently feel about my relationship?
2. Is there anything I am doing that could be impacting my relationship negatively?
3. How can I deal with our differences in a way that helps us both?

4 · Patience Problems

On a scale of 1-10, how patient are you? (Nope sorry, '0' isn't an option!)

Whilst rushing for an appointment one day, I realised the shoes that I planned to wear were already in the car. *No problem*, I thought, *I'll just chuck another pair on and change them in the car*. Once at the car I changed as planned, but in my haste I left my other pair of shoes on the roof of the car! Completely oblivious, I rolled off the drive and set off on my journey, fixated on each minute I was closer to being late.

The next thing I knew, I heard something hit the back of my car and caught a glimpse of a UFO in my rearview mirror, only for my eyes to widen as I remembered exactly where I left my shoes! I pulled over and rushed to collect a single shoe, but I was interrupted by the sound of a horn blowing at me nearby. Turning to look, and obviously frustrated, I saw a lady who was equally annoyed signalling that she wanted to turn into her driveway.

I didn't even stop to think *where* I'd pulled over, but what were the chances that the owner of that particular driveway would arrive back exactly as my shoe went rogue! I *don't have time for her impatience*, I thought (oh the irony). I proceeded to walk to where my shoe was only for her to attack her horn. As my eye began to twitch ever so slightly, I returned to my car and moved it away from her drive, before resuming the mission to retrieve my shoe.

In case you were wondering, the other shoe was back where I started in the middle of the road near my house. Yes I was late for my appointment. Yes my shoes survived. Patience - what even is that?

Looking back on that experience, I can now consider both perspectives. In my mind it would have just taken a second to grab my shoe and I had ZERO patience as I was running late, so ironically I was annoyed at the lady's lack of consideration and the fact that *she* wasn't being very patient at all! Looking at it from the other side though, I had no idea what her situation was and she had no idea where I was going. From her point of view I could have been going for a nice stroll while leaving my car lovingly parked in front of her drive…
The definition of the word 'patience' is:

"The capacity to accept or tolerate delay, problems, or suffering without becoming annoyed or anxious."

Rewind back to shoe-gate, and patience is the last thing either of us had on our minds in that moment. We couldn't have been more opposed to this definition if we tried! How capable would you say you are at tolerating delay, problems, or even suffering *without* becoming annoyed or anxious? Come on let's be honest, being patient is a challenge!

There are those who struggle to be patient when faced with delay - traffic especially. I admit there have been times where I've been on the verge of tearing my clothes and unleashing the hulk, all because I wanted to get to my destination without waiting unnecessarily. I think I've become more patient now though, although my husband may tell you otherwise (he knows not of what he speaks!)

Your ability to tolerate problems can often depend on the scale of the problem. For example, if you can resolve a problem yourself or with the help of others, you are likely to feel in control of the situation. On the flip side, when a problem is beyond your control it's so easy to become impatient. This can lead to you feeling stressed or even depressed in worst case scenarios.

Based on the above definition, suffering is an experience that many of us wouldn't want to associate with patience. Funny thing that, because the Latin origin of the word 'patient' actually means 'suffering'! That's certainly the way most of us feel when we have to exercise any form of patience.

What is your definition of suffering? To be on the losing side during a war and seeing your comrades fall around you, or to be part of a disease-ridden community where food is scarce? It may even be something closer to home, such as the difficult experience of losing a loved one.

The word 'suffering' is defined as follows:

"The state of undergoing pain, distress, or hardship."

With that definition in mind, I'm sure you can think of relatable personal experiences. Maybe you are even having such an experience now as you read this book...

The pain of dealing with a break up and missing the very person that you believe you need most. The distress of others forming an opinion of what happened between you both, and asking you if you're okay because they want to know the details rather than to genuinely help. The hardship of imagining life without them, and trying to recommit yourself to the friends and goals that you neglected while you were consumed with the relationship.

Now imagine experiencing all of this and being able to "accept or tolerate" what is taking place "*without* becoming annoyed or anxious". That is not just the definition of patience, but it is patience in action!

You may ask how? It sounds like a near impossible feat to be in such a position, and yet to have an attitude of patience on top of your emotions and seemingly weakened state of wellbeing. Challenging - yes, but far from impossible! It's in those moments of despair and anxiety that I find myself clinging to God even more tightly.

I don't know about you, but I know that when my life is at it's most comfortable and I feel in control, that's when I begin to lose my sense of dependence on God and instead the trust starts to shift to my own capabilities. I always try to ground myself when I feel this happening, but it's so easy for my decisions that lead to positive results to also create a sense of self-satisfaction and self-dependence.

I sometimes imagine how my life would have turned out if I had been more patient in the past. I know that my journey would have required far less emotional energy! But I also find comfort in knowing that I've learned valuable lessons despite the diversions, and I now feel like I am walking in the right direction. Patience is hard, but regret is harder.

Learning patience is a lifelong lesson, but there are small ways that you can practice this valuable trait on a day to day basis. Next time you are waiting on a call and the person doesn't respond immediately, consider that something may be happening their end that requires their attention. When that driver cuts in front of you unexpectedly and speeds ahead, just sing along to your music a little louder as you meet them at the traffic lights…

It all comes down to a willingness to work on changing your perspective to a positive outlook - ultimately learning how to refresh your outlook on life.

Your thoughts

Whether you would like to meet the right person or are currently in a relationship, in what areas are you currently finding it difficult to be patient?

It's also important to acknowledge any weaknesses you have, as they can create a barrier against you moving forward with a more positive mindset. Ask yourself the following:

1. How is my impatience affecting me right now?
2. Am I willing to stay where I am if nothing changes?
3. In what areas would I like to practice being more patient?

4. Would I describe the person I am interested in/ my significant other as a patient person?

5 · Silent Expectations

You know that experience when you hear about someone without seeing what they actually look like, and when you finally meet them they're nothing like you expected? It's a strange moment when the person you've envisioned in your head is pushed aside in favour of the real person in front of you.

The expectations we hold are often formed without intention, and it's amazing how so much of our life experience since childhood can subconsciously form solid expectations that we stand by. Before the word 'love' was even a part of your vocabulary, your expectations for relationships had already been developing. Growing up, you would have taken in everything from the way your parent/s handled relationships, to the dynamic that your friends and maybe other close family members had with their partners, to your own experiences (no matter how cringeworthy!)

All of these combined influences come together as pieces of a picture, shaping an image in your mind as to what you expect from a relationship. This doesn't just include yourself, but also the expectations that you place on the other person. Even though some of our expectations may be ingrained, we need to be intentional about how we live out our expectations, as well as how we allow them to guide the way we behave.

It's important to have expectations that can help you create a high standard in love, but as you know there are also unrealistic expectations. There's a difference between saying that you would like to meet someone who is good-looking, but also has a strong moral code and would like to have children in future, to saying that you would like to meet someone who has a ripped physique, is no shorter than 6ft with a minimum salary of 40k, and loves to cook and clean.

I mean never say never, there may be some of you who are married to the latter, but the point is that your expectations can severely limit your potential to be genuinely happy with the right person, because they can't quite force themselves into your box.

Learning how to work with your expectations is so important to the way that you go about maintaining your relationship, as you can end up swaying between settling for less than you deserve and having unrealistic expectations.

What kind of relationship do you want to have?
The earlier you can ask yourself this question, the better! Ideally, when you first start developing an interest in the idea of getting into a relationship with someone else. Being single is the best time to get your head in the right place, before considering the romantic potential of someone else. Even if you are in a steady relationship right now, this question still applies to you. It's never too late to ask yourself what you want from your relationship, and to think proactively about what you can do to make positive changes.

This is also a good test to see what your relationship is actually made of, and you may have to face some hard truths that you've been avoiding for the sake of staying right where you are. If you aren't married, don't feel as though you're destined to walk that road with the person you are currently with, no matter how heavy the expectation may be from those around you. This might be a difficult thing to consider, but I'd rather encourage these thoughts now before you choose to commit to a difficult life. "Until death do us part" is a long time!

I'll never forget during our pre-marital counselling when we were asked how we would deal with the idea of separation rather than marriage if either of us felt that we were heading in different directions. There was a huge lump in my throat as this thought crossed my mind, because who wants to think about their relationship failing! The more I considered it, I had to swallow my expectations and admit that I would have to respect the reason why either of us believed that marriage wasn't the right option for us both. As heartbreaking as it would have been to experience, you can't force genuine love and a willingness to stand by another person exclusively for the rest of your lives.

I think it's so important that we remind those closest to us that it's okay to say "no" or change your mind if something doesn't feel right. Often we aren't just contending with our own expectations that we will both live happily ever after, but the expectations of those around us who don't see us anywhere else but married. I always say to my husband that anyone can get married. The real testament to your relationship comes years after the wedding with decades of true, committed love and appreciation - hopefully well into old age!

Don't get swept up in your feelings and expect to meet Mr or Mrs Right through sheer panic at the thought of being alone forever. Getting into a relationship knowing full well that you are settling will never be something that you can convince yourself feels right. There will always be something that feels slightly off, and I'm talking from experience. The valuable thing about past experiences, no matter how negative, is that they make a good thing even sweeter when it comes your way.

It's easy to underestimate just how influential our expectations are to the success of any relationship. The expectations you may have, even subconsciously, could be the reason why you are struggling in your relationship right now. Maybe your expectations are reasonable but your partner still isn't willing to meet them. You could then find yourself hanging on in the hope that things will change.

It's also key to mention that the expectations shouldn't begin and end with your partner, but you also need to have expectations for yourself too. You may feel annoyed when your partner isn't meeting your expectations, but what are you doing to meet theirs? Could you be adding to the problem without even realising?

Setting yourself clear expectations should be part of your self-care routine. Many of us can spend ages in the mirror getting ready physically, but time spent caring for our mental wellbeing is often missed when it should be considered an invaluable priority.

Taking the time to discover your innermost thoughts, feelings and challenges, will help you to understand yourself in ways that will encourage you to prioritise the right things. If you fail to reflect and *understand you* better, you'll find it hard to recognise those patterns that pull you back into the same, tiring cycle.

Life has a way of teaching you lessons whether you like it or not, but there are many situations in your life where you have the room to do the learning in advance and hopefully save yourself the heartache.

Your thoughts

Take a few minutes to write out a list of what your expectations are for your ideal partner and relationship. This may be the first time you have ever done this, but it is really helpful to understand your general attitude towards relationships. List your expectations under the following categories:

- Career
- Children
- Communication
- Faith
- Finances
- Housework
- Leisure
- Quality time

This is also a good activity to get a partner to do if you are currently in a relationship. Note down your expectations separately, then share what you've come up with once finished. This will most likely raise some important areas for discussion to help make sure you are both on the same page.

When discovering your *personal* expectations, the following questions will help to get you started:

1. What kind of person would I like to be in my relationship?
2. What might be currently preventing me from becoming that person?
3. What are the top three things that I am looking for in a significant other?
4. If my significant other is also looking for those qualities or similar, are they likely to find them in me? If not, what can I do to strengthen those areas where possible?

6 · I Love Me, I Love Me Not

As I looked in the mirror at my body a few days after giving birth, I felt the soft pouch of my belly that was no longer home to my little baby girl. I turned slightly and saw the stretch marks either side of my waist. I looked myself up and down, and then I smiled…

My body had just completed a miraculous process, and I was so proud of what I saw looking back at me! *Be kind to yourself*, I reminded myself as I looked over at my precious girl, sleeping softly following her feed. I'll be honest, there was a brief moment where I felt the urge to criticise my body, but instead I chose to be *grateful.*

I can't quite put into words how having a child changes your whole life for the better, and that change includes a refresh of your entire mindset. Suddenly the little things are so much more meaningful as you watch this tiny person learn and grow, day by day. Some changes can be harder for some people to accept than others, such as the way your body adjusts through pregnancy and after you've given birth.

Whether you've generally experienced any significant changes to your body or not, you can't swap it for another! This is where the idea of 'changing what you can and accepting what you can't change' can be a helpful lesson to learn, with those changes being within reason. For example, your change may involve hitting the gym or taking up some form of exercise to stay in shape and maintain a good level of fitness.

Let me ask you this: *when you look in the mirror each day, what do you think of the person looking back at you?* Are you happy with what you see, or are you harsh with yourself? Maybe you even avoid mirrors unless absolutely necessary.

The way that you see yourself and the inner voice that you choose to listen to can either build up or tear apart your self-esteem. This goes so much deeper than just your opinion of yourself though, as it will directly impact the kind of person you are in a relationship, including the way you treat your partner.

Everybody wants to feel beautiful or handsome in the eyes of their partner, and there is absolutely nothing wrong with that. Where you can go wrong though, is if you rely on your partner to fill your "self-esteem glass". You should come into the relationship with your glass already filled, so that whatever your partner does for you and says to you is a bonus. Without a healthy level of self-esteem, you may not even notice a problem at first as your partner may be doing a good job at keeping your glass full. That is until you have an issue, such as your partner no longer being as affectionate as you would like, then you may start to question your worth in your partner's eyes - especially if you don't voice your feelings or nothing changes.

It's unfair to rely on your partner to be the one to define your self-esteem, but at the same time this isn't an excuse for someone to treat you however they please. The great thing about having strong self-esteem, is that you'll recognise your worth when you love yourself just the way you are. It will be hard for just anyone to capture your attention romantically, and even though at times you may feel uncertain, you won't settle for anything less than you know you deserve in the long run.

I know this because my journey hasn't been a smooth one, and I've certainly had times where I've been harsh on the person looking back in the mirror. I've had different experiences where I've been getting to know guys with intention (not at the same time might I add, before you hiss at me when you pass me on the street!), and allowed myself to compromise on the things that I saw as important for the sake of just wanting to experience a relationship.

So what changed?

Learning to make time for prayer, self-reflection and practicing gratitude helped a lot, and I *chose* to be kind to the person I saw in the mirror. It was strange at first - it's so easy to analyse what you see until negativity becomes the natural conclusion, but the more I looked at myself and smiled, the more positive I began to feel. I learned how to build on the satisfaction that I was enough in my own right, without the need for validation from someone else.

Self-esteem is a daily journey and some days may not feel as rosy as others, but if your ultimate goal is to *be kind to yourself* then you'll be encouraged by how much easier it is to face each day with a sense of appreciation.

With the right person by your side for life, you'll experience vulnerability like never before. One area that often suffers when you or your partner has low self-esteem is your sex life. If you don't believe that you are desirable, then someone else is going to have a hard time convincing you otherwise. With sex being the strongest act of intimacy that two people can share with one another, it's crucial to recognise the importance of learning to love who you are.

An interesting thought is that many people use 'self-esteem' and 'self-confidence' interchangeably. Did you know that they are actually very different? You can meet a person who seems to radiate self-confidence, but yet they struggle with low self-esteem. You just may not know it because you don't see it! Celebrities are perfect examples, as there are those who appear confident in front of a camera, yet suffer from extremely low self-esteem.

Self-esteem can also be defined as the personal "estimate" that someone gives themselves, based on their perception of their own worth. Self-confidence in contrast is largely based on your abilities. When you are progressing in a job or have developed a new skill, you'll develop confidence in what you are capable of achieving. Self-confidence is based upon what I can do, whereas self-esteem is based upon who I am.

Self-esteem can grow as a result of self-confidence, but because it is a deeper issue it tends to affect the very core of your view on life. Many of those deeper issues often come from your childhood and experience in school, which has shaped the way you view yourself and your assumptions over the way others view you.

Imagine the following scenario:

You are with your partner and some mutual friends, and you hear your partner joking with one of them about the fact that you never get anywhere on time. Although you were smiling at the time, you felt very awkward, so you confront your partner about this later on when you have the opportunity to talk privately.

Your partner doesn't understand what the big deal is, and you end up arguing out of frustration. You start to consider the fact that you probably overreacted, and you both manage to put what happened behind you and move on rather than addressing what happened, or more importantly addressing *why you reacted in the way that you did.*

Without dealing with the root of the problem, you are likely to fall back into the same situation again and again. Instead of just brushing off what happened, consider why you reacted in the way that you did. Clearly it was more than the fact that your partner was joking about you always being late (you probably already know that yourself), but it possibly had more to do with the fact that he was joking about it in public with someone else. It may have felt as though he was making fun of you. This could then cause you to subconsciously react, especially if you had childhood experiences where others would also make fun of you. Maybe you were even a victim of bullying...

Even if you can't relate to this particular scenario, it's an example of how there are often hidden issues that cause us to act the way we do. Unless we are willing to get uncomfortable and deal with any issues, we'll always end up right back where we started with the same stressful feelings.

When you look at your life from the perspective of an adult, and rationally address the feelings that you had as a child that are most likely associated to the experiences you are having now, then you can work on turning those weaknesses into strengths.

The ability to reach this point has a lot to do with your self-esteem, which is why it's so important to consider what could be currently holding you back. As you learn to love yourself no less than you deserve, then you can also experience real love shared with someone else in the way that you both deserve.

Your thoughts

A healthy sense of self-esteem, or a high "estimate" of personal worth, can create a huge difference in any relationship. Consider the following questions:

1. If someone compliments you on your appearance, do you believe what they say? Or do you brush off the comment?
2. If your partner was to talk to you about an issue that they have with you, would you be able to listen? Or would it be more likely to cause an argument?
3. If you heard that someone had been talking about you behind your back, would you let the comments slide because you're yet to hear it from the source, or would you be more likely to react out of anger?

There is a deeper meaning behind every little thing that we do or say, no matter how insignificant it may seem. Don't be afraid to dig deeper, as it will encourage a stronger sense of growth and understanding that will help solidify the foundation of your relationship.

7 · Good-Looking Personality

There's something so attractive about a life partner who supports your dreams and is your loudest cheerleader!

On the way to work one morning, I was speaking to my husband when he told me that he was proud of the effort I was making to reach my goals. Rewind to a month or so before, and the conversation on this topic went a little differently. I had all the creative ideas to share, but he was honest about the fact that he was yet to see me making a consistent effort to make those ideas a reality.

I think my turning point came when I turned 25 (just after I got married and pre-baby), and I began to review all of the things I had wanted to achieve by that age. Not a lot had changed. The last thing I wanted was for my goals to still be 'pending' when I turned 30 (only 3 years to go at the time of writing this!)

My journey would have been so much harder if my husband wasn't supportive of me. We had our differences when I was considering whether to leave the role I was in at that time, but we came together in the end and took a team approach to the challenges ahead. Experiences like this remind me of how beneficial it is to be in a relationship with someone who has a good-looking personality.

Never take a man for granted who is willing to not only support you, but to go out of his way for you. A man who has chosen to pursue you above all others. A man who isn't afraid to lead, or to be completely honest with you. A man who chooses to be vulnerable around you and trusts you with his whole heart.

The dynamic of your relationship is established long before you make things "official". Even if stress levels are high, healthy relationships consist of two people working with each other to stay united, rather than reaching the point where they break apart. If you have reached this point on more than one occasion and it is still early days, you seriously need to question whether this is what you want for the rest of your life.

In a world where so many lives are run by social media, it can be hard to see beyond the persona that someone chooses for themselves. Captivated by the beauty of precisely planned or edited content, is it any wonder why so many people have a shallow concept of love? Nowadays we don't even need to know someone personally to know a little too much about them! Privacy is no longer a priority and ironically, it is one of the most vital parts of a wholesome relationship.

The "like-mind" is one that dominates our culture, with the ability to click on a button and show your appreciation through liking/sharing now considered to be a second-nature to us, but is this seemingly effortless action capable of causing more harm than good?

I had a conversation with a friend about this, where he told me about his experience when he shared an encouraging post on Facebook. After checking back every now and again, he saw that his post still hadn't received any 'likes'. An hour passed by and there was still no activity, so he considered deleting the post completely. It was only when he thought about his reasons for sharing the post in the first place, that he was able to accept leaving it up on his page whether people clicked the 'like' button or not.

I'm sure there are many of us who can relate to this. If we are used to seeing people 'liking' the content we post, then it can be difficult to accept when this doesn't happen or if we don't get as much attention as we'd like. There are many of us who would go ahead and delete the post if there was a lack of public affirmation, but why?

As in the case of my friend, he had to consider why he posted his content in the first place. We measure things according to the actions that we see in the form of liking/sharing, but what about the actions that we do not see? We never know how effective our seemingly small attempts to reach out can be, and this is something that we need to keep in mind in order to maintain a stable mindset and remain consistent in what we set out to accomplish.

The hardest thing is learning how to recognise the opinions of others without allowing them to define you as an individual. If you were to post a picture of yourself, and just one person liked the picture, how would you feel? If you are someone who is used to receiving many 'likes' and then this happened, then you would probably assume that you were experiencing a technical error and remove it to repost again. In contrast, if you are someone who doesn't necessarily use social media then this probably wouldn't bother you. You may think that someone deleting a post for lack of 'likes' is excessive, but I can say that I've done it.

I found myself spending *ages* in order to perfect the way I looked in a single picture, and often this meant taking picture after picture until I was happy. I didn't stop there! Next came the editing, and I spent even more time ensuring the end result was precisely what I wanted. It's only now that I can look back and recognise the lengths that I was going to, just to gain the approval of others. Society has ever changing opinions of what beauty is, and these opinions can be contagious. Simply put; the more 'likes' we receive, the more accepted we feel. This reflects on so many other aspects of our lives, and in everything that we do there is an underlying need to feel a sense of acceptance.

Now imagine how risky it is to be so caught up with this mindset and then to get into a relationship! Once you have conditioned yourself with the "like-mind" way of thinking, you can end up having a very critical approach either towards the person you are with, or concerning the perception that you think they have of you. You can fall into the trap of wrapping so much of yourself around one individual, that you lose your own individuality.

If you are considering marriage, it is important to ask yourself if the person you are planning on spending the rest of your life with is willing to help you reach your goals. You may have your differences and it may take some discussion before you are on the same page, but when you are it is the most fulfilling feeling. If one hurdle in your path is enough to make you give up on what you want to achieve, then maybe you don't want it enough...

This all sounds encouraging, but what do you do when your partner instead attacks your goals or just isn't willing to listen? How can you take a team approach with someone who isn't interested in working as a team?

If this is your reality, then it will probably help to sit down and review where you are and where you want to go, and start making things happen! If you can do something to change whatever is making you miserable and draining your motivation out of each day, then what are you waiting for?

I thank God for my husband, truly, as he reminds me of my potential when I question what I have to offer. A strong relationship consists of two people cheering each other on through life and holding each other up when things get tough. If you take one thing from this book, it's a reminder that you shouldn't settle for anything less than a true team spirit in your relationship.

Your thoughts

Are you currently struggling with the "like-mind" way of thinking? It might help to take a break from social media and spend some time doing the things you enjoy without the pressure of analysing your every move.

Consider the following questions:

1. Am I using my time wisely?
2. What can I do to make reaching my long-term goals a reality?
3. Are there any goals that I am yet to share with my partner? If so, why?
4. When I share content online, what is my thought process behind the content I post?

5.   When was the last time I took a break from social media, and just appreciated the reality of each moment?

Take a walk in the park, meet up with a friend, do something fun with the one you love… just don't let your life fly by without making the most of each opportunity to appreciate life for all it can be!

8 · Let Me Love You

We love feeling comfortable. Fact.

The idea of wearing a fitted dress or a tailored suit whilst enjoying a lazy day at home, isn't as appealing as throwing on a pair of jogging bottoms and a baggy t-shirt. Neither is the idea of attending a party by yourself where you don't know anyone but the host, as appealing as attending a party where you're greeted by familiar faces.

Our comfort zone often defines our actions; including what we are willing to do and what we won't do, where we are willing to go and where we won't to go. Whatever the circumstance, the level of comfort we experience will play a role in the outcome of many situations. Despite having such a positive meaning, comfort isn't always a good thing…

It was probably news to my husband to hear that I didn't need to be spoiled with birthday gifts for me to appreciate the occasion. There was a time where he was between jobs and he wanted to mark my birthday in a special way, but I knew that funds were tight. Don't get me wrong, it's lovely to be treated! At that time though, the reality of our financial situation was my main consideration. He still felt like he was letting me down, and even though our expectations were different, we found a way to meet in the middle.

Most women are especially sensitive to important dates and celebrations such as birthdays, anniversaries etc. She expects him to make just as much as an effort for her as she would for him, if not more so. Whereas some men love to impress their partners, but are more relaxed when it comes to their own birthdays. Then there are some men who are just relaxed either way!

Issues usually arise when expectations are not expressed, or met. There can also be a point of contention when these expectations are met to begin with, but become less of a priority as the years go by. I can't speak from experience on maintaining your marriage twenty years down the line, but I can speak from experience on what I see around me.

Many people fail to realise the risks of becoming too comfortable over the long term. Some partners have learned to be content that things are no longer the way they were, but what about those who refuse to accept this change? This is a common point of conflict, and both the perception of your partner and the overall essence of your relationship can change completely as a result.

There are certain aspects of your relationship that will inevitably change over the years, due to various responsibilities that take priority (career, children etc.), alongside your physical health/age, but relationships that maintain their consistency should be made up of two people who are willing to leave their comfort zones for each other. It's the little things that matter; like making a conscious effort to set apart quality time, leaving little reminders that he/she is loved, and looking after your physical appearance.

The demands of life can cloud these small efforts, and we can end up so busy that our relationship ends up suffering. The more we break free of our comfort zones and start making more of an effort, the more we will become far more sensitive to the wants, needs, and desires of our partner. When both people have this mindset, they create a beautifully wholesome experience! Unfortunately many relationships instead consist of a one-sided approach, where only one person is willing to put in the effort while the other sits comfortably.

It should be your priority to start as you mean to go on. Don't wait until you're married to start implementing positive changes and routines. If you have concerns now - address them. If nothing changes - move on. I know it may not be as simple as that when you're emotionally invested in someone else, but the principle really is as blunt as that. Anything that may be concerning to you now will only become a raging issue within your marriage if you leave it. That and the fact that you will be tied to this person with their issues for the rest of your life!

The special truth about relationships is that they are what you make them. There's nothing quite like getting to know a person inside and out, and having someone in your life that knows you inside and out (sometimes even better than you know yourself!)

The biggest battle we will ever face is against ourselves. Those selfish wants, desires, and expectations that can turn even the sweetest of relationships sour. There is nothing wrong with having personal wants, desires, and expectations as these can all be very positive! However there is a problem when we think selfishly while involved in a relationship, which of itself requires selflessness and unity. You can't hope to have a healthy relationship when you're only in it for what you can get from the other person.

During my teenage years in particular, I was exposed to every kind of relationship. I didn't have to be personally involved in them to be exposed to them, and I saw many variations from my friends, to my family, to complete strangers. What I was seeing stood out to me during those years of my life - primarily because I was beginning to learn what it meant to actually be in a relationship. I remember moments where I would long to be a part of the "love trend" at school, but the way people behaved when they were together would also put me off the idea.

Since childhood, our surroundings have influenced the way we learn and grow. Some of those lessons may have been difficult, but they have ultimately shaped our understanding of life. This is why the challenges you may have faced as a child at home, can end up determining the way you conduct yourself in relationships.

Consider this: *"When you were younger, and began to develop a genuine interest in the opposite sex, what were your reasons for wanting to enter into a relationship?"*

You may need to think long and hard, or you maybe you answered straight away. Regardless, I'm asking you this question with a focus on your experiences *then* rather than now, as your understanding of romantic relationships as a child would have been at a basic level. There are those who hardly progress much further from this stage, which is why dysfunctional relationships are so common.

When relationships were formed during your childhood, they most probably started with someone saying "he fancies her", or "she fancies him". Such comments are often perceived as 'cute', or 'sweet', but under the surface you'll see how we are exposed to experiences that impact our judgement, long before we even develop an interest in the opposite sex.

An online search of the word "fancy" came up with the following definitions:

Verb - *feel a desire or liking for*

Noun - 1. a superficial or transient feeling of liking or attraction

2. the faculty of imagination

Synonyms - desire, urge, wish, want

The word "fancy" is even defined as "superficial", so in other words it only appears to be real until examined more closely. This is typical of shallow relationships that usually struggle to go the distance, as there isn't much holding them together. Love isn't mentioned anywhere in this definition, and it is clear to see how selfish the word really is in the context of a relationship.

The story usually goes like this. I desire him, or have an urge to be with her, but once we get into the relationship and the journey starts getting a little harder, then we lose that desire or urge and move on. Rather than acting on impulse and expecting to stay in that mindset (which can only last for so long before you run out of steam), that initial surge of attraction that makes you feel as though you can't be without that person should transition to a more rational, proactive way of thinking.

Often this is the point where a person wakes up and sees their relationship for what it truly is, which can sometimes feel like an overnight experience! As you see your relationship from all angles, it is down to no-one else but you AND your partner to put the work into shaping what you have and building for the better. You can't just expect to comfortably sit where you are without the need to put in an effort to maintain a good thing (I try to continually remind myself of this too!) That's like living in your home without ever cleaning it, then acting surprised when you see a mess around you…

So to wrap up this chapter let me ask you the following questions to encourage you proactively, whether you're currently single or not:

What has your love created?
What will your love create?

True love is impactful. Whether it allows you to reach people and encourage them in ways you never expected, or to bring new life into the world as your family grows, it's powerful to think about the kind of mark that you would like your love to leave on this world long after you're gone.

Your thoughts

In a world where being selfish is pretty much a natural way of thinking, it's beneficial to take a step back and consider how you are treating your partner (and for them to do the same!)
Are you loving them in the way that you would also like to be loved?

Ask yourself the following:

1. What can you give?
2. How can you help?
3. What can you do differently?

This way of thinking will help us not to get stuck in our comfort zones. You may even feel challenged to ask yourself or your spouse these questions on a regular basis, to remind yourself to think differently. Achieving a consistent change requires a consistent effort!

9 · Embracing Failure

Years back I was travelling with a friend, when she asked me the following question:

"How do you know if he is *the one*?"

The car was silent for a few moments while I tried to work out the best way to answer her. Nothing came to mind. All I could say to her was, "the fact that we are both in relationships yet neither of us can answer that question, is probably our answer".

I realised how easy it is to become blind when we truly want something. It's a horrible feeling to have to end a relationship, especially when you are not only emotionally invested but are also physically involved with that person. Many of us struggle to leave bad relationships behind, as we end up acting married before we are even ready to consider making such a huge commitment.

Long-term relationships can feel like the hardest to leave behind, as it's so easy to get comfortable. When someone isn't for you though, you will know it deep down. Despite everyone around you sharing their opinions of support and how good you both look together, you can't escape your own thoughts. Sooner or later, you will have to face your future with or without this person.

Fear of the unknown can be very real when considering separation, and you may worry that you might never meet another person who is willing to commit to a relationship with you for the long-term. I had that exact thought in a previous relationship, and it was that same mindset that kept me where I was for longer than I should have been, even though things weren't working out. It's easier to think such thoughts when we lack the self-esteem and faith that we may have had back when we met that person. Weaknesses in those areas can damage any relationship.

You should always feel as though you can be honest with your partner if you are unhappy about something they have done, without the fear that they will dismiss how you feel. They may not be happy to hear what you have to say, but they should be willing to listen and work past the problem regardless. Too many couples have a breakdown in communication because feelings aren't respected.

The right person will inspire you to be the best version of you. If you are struggling even to be yourself then you need to either make the necessary changes, or move on. Yes it will hurt, and people will want to know what happened (don't feel obligated to tell everyone), and you will have to get used to being single once more, but this is all part of the process of growth. It is far less painful to leave a bad relationship than it is to *stay in one for the rest of your life!*

We've all most likely had the experience where we meet a person and start to consider whether there is romantic potential or not. The moment we finally meet someone who seems to tick all of our boxes, we change our light from red to green (ain't nobody got time to wait for amber!) In reality though, so many of us struggle to set boundaries for ourselves and we are left to deal with the consequences. Even in the early days of your relationship, the way that you establish boundaries and work through problems will determine the level of partnership that you are able to build with the other person.

Everyone should wear a badge that reads "proceed with caution!" The process of getting to know someone romantically is the last thing that you want to rush, as the decision you make can either enrich or enslave you. It's as real as that. I'll be honest, when you experience the euphoria of meeting someone special it can be hard to think rationally. It's even harder to think straight when those closest to you are super excited for you! But in those moments where it's just you and your thoughts, it helps to reflect on your experience of getting to know this person and pinpoint any concerns you may have (if any).

While getting to know my husband, I appreciated being able to see who he was in so many different environments and see the type of relationships he had with other people. From his family home, to church, to social time with friends, to his grandparent's homes, to my family home - I can't tell you how valuable it is to see all of the sides of the person you are considering romantically.

The more we learned about each other, the easier it was to be vulnerable with each other and talk about any issues we had. Comparing the experience of getting to know my husband with previous experiences, I was able to see how I was completely at ease this time around to when I previously questioned my every move. Experience has taught me that if you have to ask questions about something - pay attention. We never ask ourselves if we should get dressed in the morning or if we should travel to work, as these are just routine aspects of our day that happen almost without thinking. On the flip side, we would question ourselves about whether we should have worn that dress if it felt a little too short, or if we should have still driven the car after it started making strange noises.

Pay attention to your uncertainty, as when something is happening naturally without you feeling the need to question each move, then you'll know you're exactly where you should be.

It's easy to lean the other way and feel as though what you have with this person is too good to be true. This happens especially if you have had your trust broken in the past, or if this is your first serious relationship. We can be our own worst enemies and self-sabotage a good thing because deep down we either don't believe we are deserving of what we have with this person, or we struggle to believe they have genuinely good intentions.

After negative experiences, I adopted the attitude that I would always try and be trusting until that person gave me a reason to think otherwise. I still have to remind myself of this, as sometimes the stories that we tell ourselves start to impact our opinion of the person we are with when they have done absolutely nothing wrong! That is why trust is such a huge part of being able to maintain a healthy relationship, and part of that is learning to accept the things that are beyond your control (within reason of course).

If something is genuinely going well for you, then be grateful. Based on past relationships, many of us fear any sense of failure, but you can't determine what happens tomorrow even if you tried. When you have a good thing, try and find your contentment in what you have while you have it.

Have you ever had a great experience where something seemed to be going so well, only for it to end in failure?

A job interview where you left feeling as though you made a great impression, only to hear that you had been unsuccessful. A relationship that seemed to show all the right signs of long-term potential, only for things to turn sour. The effort of consistently trying to develop financial stability, only to see your savings disappear to pay off rising debts.

Life is full of these moments, and the easiest thing to do is to admit defeat. In a world where five people at random are likely to describe you in five different ways based on looks alone, it is damaging to fall into the routine of allowing your experiences to define you. Everywhere you go, people will have their own opinion of you based on how you think, look, act, talk and dress. You can't escape the perceptions of others! Someone may comment that they think you look lovely in an outfit, but based on the way that someone else is looking at you, you may start to feel self-conscious.

Similarly, I've realised that some companies might recognise my skills and offer me an opportunity to join them, whereas others may instead offer someone else the position based on them having a little more experience. We should never allow someone else to define how talented we are, or for us to question our ability to the point where we fall away from doing what we love.

If we didn't fail, then we wouldn't learn to appreciate the true value of all that we have to offer. Your belief in your ability, and your confidence in who you are and where your strength comes from, needs to remain solid regardless of what others may say.

This chapter is not about providing instructions on how to break up with someone, but instead I'm encouraging you to consider how the failure of an unhealthy relationship can actually lead to something positive that far exceeds your expectations. You can't always fix what has been broken, and that may lead you to leave your current relationship in the past. Through my own journey I have found encouragement in my relationship with God, and He has taught me how to leave the pain in the past and free myself for the promise of a better future.

Your thoughts

When was the last time you took a moment to sit and reflect? Take some time to ask yourself the following questions about a potential or existing partner:

1. Are they of the same culture? Or is there a divide? (I say divide because there are many people who come together of different cultures and get along smoothly, but this can also be an area of major conflict later on. This can happen especially if there is a desire to move countries and live elsewhere etc.)
2. How do they relate to your family members, and how comfortable are their family around you?
3. When managing finances, are they able to save money and spend it wisely?
4. Can you discuss topics such as finance, boundaries, and any habits or issues that you feel need to be addressed, openly and honestly with them?
5. Can you work together on everyday tasks if required?

These are just a few questions, and I encourage you to come up with some of your own. These questions are based on my experiences so far, and I've learned how beneficial it is to be able to think realistically about how each question relates to the other person.

Look beyond the way they make you feel, and find out what your relationship is really made of. It's far better that you uncover these things now, than find yourself struggling to deal with deep-rooted issues in the years to come.

10 · Happily Ever Before

Around Christmas time, I remember a particular car journey where I ended up tuning in to hear an interesting conversation on the radio. It went something like this:

Presenter: "So at the moment we have a guest counsellor on the show. She will be answering any questions that you have concerning challenges you may be facing over the Christmas period. We will need your help with this next one!

"Here is the dilemma: this listener has a boyfriend who is planning to propose to her on Christmas day. The only reason she knows this is because she asked her parents to tell her if he ever asked their permission to marry her. She doesn't feel she is ready for marriage, but she doesn't want to say 'no' and hurt his feelings. Let us know your thoughts, and we'll see what we can do to help this listener. We'll be right back after the break."

break for ads

Presenter: "Before the break, we shared an interesting dilemma. We thought we needed a bit more information, so we've managed to get hold of the person directly. Hi there!"

Caller: "Hello"

Presenter: "So tell us a bit more about your situation. We've had quite a few suggestions from other listeners - one idea is to watch a romantic film with your boyfriend and talk about the fact that you don't like the idea of marriage."

Caller: "I have already told him a few times, but he doesn't seem to get the message."

Presenter: "Do you love him?"

Caller: "Of course. We've been together for nine years and I like things the way they are."

Presenter: "So why don't you want to marry him?"

Caller: "I'm only 25 and I'm happy. I might consider marriage when I'm older, but right now I don't see why things need to change."

Presenter: "Well the general feedback from listeners is that you should tell him sooner rather than later. Christmas is only a couple of weeks away!"

Caller: "I know, but how do I tell him without revealing that my parents told me he was planning to propose."

Presenter: "You don't have to mention your parents, just bring up the topic of marriage and make it clear that you don't want to get married. Maybe you should also question *why* he wants to get married. If things are fine as they are, then he should respect how you feel… Let's find out what our guest counsellor thinks."

Counsellor: "I would disagree. I think you should be honest and tell him that you parents told you."

Presenter: "Really?"

Counsellor: "It would be obvious that you know something, especially as you would be discussing marriage so close to his plans for the proposal. You always end up in a worse situation when you try to lie to soften the blow, so just be honest. Tell him that you asked your parents to tell you if he ever asked for their permission to marry you, so they told you about his plans to propose on Christmas day. Let him know that you aren't ready."

Presenter: "... and that's why she's the counsellor! Is that helpful advice?"

Caller: "Hmm I guess... but who proposes to someone in their living room anyway?"

Presenter: "Would you prefer if he took you to the top of the Eiffel Tower?"

Caller: "At least that would be romantic."
Presenter: *Laughing* "At last the truth comes out!"

I was intrigued to hear how this caller was so reluctant to get married after being in a relationship for so long. I'm sure there were many listening who thought she was being ridiculous, and felt more sympathy towards her partner for his seemingly wasted efforts. On the other side though, there were probably also listeners who were able to relate to the way she felt about marriage. *Where do you stand?*

Many of us are skeptical of marriage, especially if we have never experienced or witnessed healthy examples. We live in a society where the idea of "loving" your partner even though you may not trust them is encouraged. When we experience difficulties, it's no wonder that the thought of a happy marriage is considered little more than a fairytale.

An eagerness to find our "happily ever after" can lead us to a place where we're craving happiness itself. There are those who spend a lifetime trying to figure out what they want and where they are going, when they just need to learn how to be genuinely happy and content with who they are and what they have. Anything else that comes will then feel like an added bonus.

For a start, happiness begins with you. I can't stress this enough! If you are placing your happiness on hold until you meet Mr or Mrs Right, then you're placing an unfair responsibility on that potential person to define your happiness. What if he or she never comes? Before you throw this book out the window, hear me out.

Even though the idea of not meeting someone to share your life with may be a scary thought, what's even scarier is *putting your life on hold* with no guarantee that you will meet someone. Some people spend so long in a state of misery, that they place so much pressure on the person they meet to *finally* make them happy! Many relationships turn ugly when one person is relying on the other to provide their happiness.

Happiness comes before a relationship. Repeat that to yourself. There are couples who are miserable and married, longing for the days when they were single. When you learn how to be happy by yourself, if someone worthwhile comes into your life then they will add to your happiness, instead of trying to make and keep you happy. The same goes for your partner, and if they are also content in themselves then you will be a bonus to their life.

Despite any challenges, the encouraging truth is that it's never too late to stand back and take some time to consider how you can work on your happiness. Whether you are seriously considering marriage or are yet to enter into a relationship, the most important thing you can do for yourself is to work on being happy and content *before* sharing your life with someone else.

My experiences in love have taught me that it's okay to recognise your mistakes. In fact, that's the only way that you can learn and do better the next time around.

Failing tests your resolve. Failing strengthens your optimism and encourages positive thinking. Failing teaches you patience, understanding and resilience.

Failing in love may be hard, but learning about and experiencing what true love is despite failing is the most incredible feeling...

I'll leave you with this single question:

What makes you happy?

List your 'Top 10' answers and remind yourself often. The happier you are, the easier it will be to share the best version of yourself with that special someone.

Don't worry, be happy! *Breaks into song*

Printed by Amazon Italia Logistica S.r.l.
Torrazza Piemonte (TO), Italy

11121362R00034